I LIKE DUCKS

All Year Long

CAROLYN WILD

Wild Acres Books

Spallumcheen, British Columbia, Canada

Published by Wild Acres Books
Spallumcheen, BC, Canada
https://wildacresbooks.ca/

Find more children's books, giveaways, colouring pages and worksheets at:

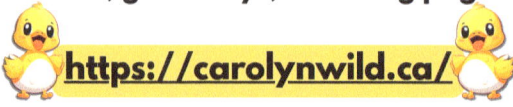

I Like Ducks: All Year Long (Wild Acres Farm Series - Book 1)

Perfect for independent readers ages 4–7, this charming counting book also makes a fun read-aloud for younger children to build early literacy skills.

Word Count: 39	**Page Count: 26**	**PM Readers: 3 - 4 Red**
Guided Reading Level: C-D	**Lexile Range: BR190L- 0L**	**ATOS LEVEL: 1.0**

Explore more about emergent readers, literacy development, and early learning at Carolyn Wild's website: https://carolynwild.ca/

Carolyn Wild – Author, Designer, Photographer
Geoff Wild - Editor, Webmaster

ISBN 978-1-998062-05-8 (eBook)
ISBN 978-1-998062-00-3 (Paperback)

This book is dedicated to my husband, Geoff, for his patience, his understanding, and for letting me have so many wonderful animals on our farm.

I like ducks.

I like ducks in the spring.

I like ducks in the summer.

I like ducks in the fall.

I like ducks in the winter.

I like ducks in the water.

I like ducks in the tub!

High-Frequency Sight Words

water

ducks

spring

tub

summer

fall

winter

The Life Cycle of a Duck

egg

hatchling

duckling

juvenile

adult

The Four Seasons

Match the seasons to the pictures.

fall

spring

winter

summer

Indian Runner Duck Facts

Indian Runner ducks are excellent egg layers and were first bred in China about 2,000 years ago. Farmers used them in rice fields to eat pests like snails, insects, and weeds, and to clean up leftover grain.

Dutch explorers called them 'Penguin Ducks' because they stand upright like penguins, which helps them run instead of waddle. This unique body shape makes them fast and agile.

Indian Runner ducks are adaptable to both hot and cold weather and are currently on the recovery list with the Livestock Conservancy

READ MORE

https://livestockconservancy.org/
heritage-breeds/heritage-breeds-
list/runner-duck

Learning to Read Guidelines

- Read to your child every day, starting at birth.
- Point to pictures and words while reading.
- Reinforce left-to-right reading by moving your finger under each word.
- If your child struggles with a word, help them focus on the first letter, then the middle and ending sounds.
- Encourage predictions based on the pictures.
- Let your child try to figure out the word. If needed, provide the word so they can continue reading.
- Teach sight words from the book, as these can be tricky and don't always follow phonetic patterns.
- Discuss the story and ask questions like "Who?", "What?", "When?", "Why?" and "How?".
- Give your child time to think and respond.
- Keep reading sessions short and fun—remember, reading is bonding time!

Look for more reading guidelines, books, colouring sheets, worksheets and book giveaways on this website:

https://carolynwild.ca/

Wild Acres Farm Series

Emergent Readers		Simple Sentences
Science Facts		Real Photos
Fiction & Nonfiction		Picture Dictionary
Interactive		Rhyming
Large Font		Sight Words
Leveled Books		Rebus Clues

Carolyn Wild, a primary teacher with over 25 years of experience, lives with her husband, Geoff, on Wild Acres farm in the Okanagan, BC, Canada. While teaching, she creates engaging picture books that combine real photos and illustrations to make learning fun and accessible, covering literacy, math, science, and social studies.

Inspired by farm life, student needs, and the Okanagan landscape, Carolyn's Wild Acres Farm Series encourages children to explore their world. The leveled readers teach key skills like sight words, counting, rhymes, and science facts, with picture dictionaries and guided reading tips that foster a love of learning at home and in classrooms.

You can visit the Wild Acres farm website: https://wildacres.ca

Connect with the Author

Website
https://carolynwild.ca/

Facebook
@WildAcresBooks

Instagram
@carolynwildauthor

Pinterest
@carolynwildauthor

Dear Reader,

I'm so glad you and your little ones are enjoying my books! If you have a moment, I'd be grateful if you could leave a review.

What did you or your children enjoy most about the book? A simple rating or review on the store's website, Goodreads, or my website would mean so much to me and help others discover the story.

Thank you so much for your support! I can't wait to hear what you think.

Warmly,
Carolyn Wild